Krishna Chalisa

Published in Sanskriti Press
Rupa Publications India Pvt. Ltd 2025
7/16, Ansari Road, Daryaganj
New Delhi 110002

Sales centres:
Bengaluru Chennai
Hyderabad Jaipur Kathmandu
Kolkata Mumbai Prayagraj

Copyright © Rupa Publications India Pvt. Ltd 2025

All rights reserved.
No part of this publication may be reproduced, transmitted,
or stored in a retrieval system, in any form or by any means,
electronic, mechanical, photocopying, recording or otherwise,
without the prior permission of the publisher.

P-ISBN: 978-93-7003-610-9
E-ISBN: 978-93-7003-171-5

First impression 2025

10 9 8 7 6 5 4 3 2 1

Printed in India

This book is sold subject to the condition that it shall not, by way of
trade or otherwise, be lent, resold, hired out, or otherwise circulated,
without the publisher's prior consent, in any form of binding or
cover other than that in which it is published.

Contents

Introduction / 5

Chalisa / 9

श्री कृष्ण आरती / 97

Shri Krishna Aarti / 100

Introduction

The **Krishna Chalisa**, a sacred hymn dedicated to Lord Krishna, carries within it the vibrancy of devotion and the divine playfulness that characterize the god himself. For centuries, it has been a source of spiritual solace and inspiration for millions. Every verse of the Chalisa echoes the enchanting melody of Krishna's flute, invoking not only his divine attributes but also his compassionate nature, his boundless love, and his timeless wisdom. In the repetitive recitation of these verses, devotees seek a deep connection with Krishna, yearning for his blessings and guidance in their lives.

It is undeniable that the Krishna Chalisa holds a profound significance in the hearts of those who chant it. As the hymn's words flow, they bring to life the divine figure of Krishna—who is not just a god of power and might, but also a compassionate friend, a loving guide, and a protector of all who seek refuge. The chanting of the Chalisa acts as a bridge between the devotee and the deity, creating an intimate space for surrender and devotion. The more one chants, the more Krishna's divine presence is felt, imbuing the soul with peace and joy.

But what is it that makes the Krishna Chalisa so transformative? For many, it is more than just a prayer—it is a means of diving into the depths of Krishna's multifaceted persona. His playful leelas (divine pastimes), his teachings in the Bhagavad Gita, and his role as the protector of his devotees come alive in each line of the Chalisa. The devotion it inspires is not about formality or ritual; rather, it is a personal and heartwarming connection with the god who danced with gopis in Vrindavan, lifted the mountain of Govardhan, and revealed the path to liberation in the Gita.

The rhythmic flow of the verses serves as a gentle reminder of Krishna's divine nature, allowing one to release the burdens of life and enter a state of tranquility. With each chant, there is a sense of being drawn into Krishna's embrace, finding comfort in his love and guidance.

The Krishna Chalisa, therefore, is not merely a series of chants—it is an invitation. An invitation to join in Krishna's divine dance, to experience his boundless love, and to be uplifted by his eternal wisdom. Through this hymn, Krishna's presence is not just called upon, but actively experienced, offering devotees a path to peace, joy, and divine grace.

Chalisa

|| दोहा ||

बंशी शोभित कर मधुर, नील जलद तन श्याम।
अरुणअधरजनु बिम्बफल, नयनकमलअभिराम।।

Banshi shobhit kar madhur,
neel jalad tan shyaam.
Arunadhara janum bimbaphal,
nayankamalabhiram.

The flute adorns his lips with sweetness, his body is dark like the blue clouds. His face, like a red lotus, and his eyes are delightful like the lotus.

पूर्ण इन्द्र, अरविन्द मुख, पीताम्बर शुभ साज।
जय मनमोहन मदन छवि, कृष्णचन्द्र महाराज।।

Purn Indra, Arvind mukh, peetambar shubh saaj.
Jai Manmohan Madan chavi, Krishnachandra Maharaj.

He is the complete Indra, with a face like a lotus, wearing a yellow robe, and his attire is auspicious.
Victory to the enchanting one, the one with the beauty of Cupid, Lord Krishna, the king of the moon.

जय यदुनंदन जय जगवंदन।
जय वसुदेव देवकी नन्दन॥

Jai Yadunandan Jai Jagavandan.
Jai Vasudev Devaki Nandan.

Victory to the son of Yadu, victory to the
Lord of the world.
Victory to Vasudev's son, the son of
Devaki.

जय यशुदा सुत नन्द दुलारे।
जय प्रभु भक्तन के दृग तारे।।

Jai Yashoda sut nand dulare.
Jai Prabhu bhaktan ke drig tare.

Victory to the son of Yashoda, the beloved of Nand.
Victory to the Lord, the star of the eyes of his devotees.

जय नट-नागर, नाग नथइया।।
कृष्ण कन्हइया धेनु चरइया।।

Jai Nat-Nagar, Naag Nathaiya.
Krishna Kanhiya Dhenucharaiya.

Victory to the Lord of dancers, the Lord of serpents.
Krishna, the cowherd, who grazes the cattle.

पुनि नख पर प्रभु गिरिवर धारो।
आओ दीनन कष्ट निवारो।।

*Puni nakh par prabhu girivar dhaaro.
Aao deenan kasht nivaaro.*

The Lord holds the mountain on his finger.
Come, remove the sufferings of the poor and destitute.

वंशी मधुर अधर धरि टेरौ।
होवे पूर्ण विनय यह मेरौ।।

Vanshi madhur adhar dhari terau.
Hove poorn vinay yah mero.

With the sweet flute on his lips, he calls out.
May my complete humility be accepted.

आओ हरि पुनि माखन चाखो।
आज लाज भारत की राखो।।

Aao Hari puni makhan chakho.
Aaj laaj Bharat ki rakho.

Come, O Lord, taste the butter once again.
Today, remove the shame of India.

गोल कपोल, चिबुक अरुणारे।
मृदु मुस्कान मोहिनी डारे।।

Gol kapol, chibuk arunare.
Mridu muskaan mohini daare.

With round cheeks and a reddish chin,
His soft smile captivates all hearts.

राजित राजिव नयन विशाला।
मोर मुकुट वैजन्तीमाला।।

Rajit Rajiv nayana vishala.
Mor mukut vaijantimala.

His large eyes shine like lotuses,
His crown is adorned with peacock
feathers and a garland of victory.

कुंडल श्रवण, पीत पट आछे।
कटि किंकिणी काछनी काछे।।

Kundal shravan, peet pat aache.
Kati kinkini kaachani kaache.

He wears earrings in his ears, and a yellow garment.
His waist is adorned with bells and a golden belt.

नील जलज सुन्दर तनु सोहे।
छबि लखि, सुर नर मुनिमन मोहे।।

Neel jalaj sundar tanu sohe.
Chhabi lakhi, sur nar muniman mohe.

His beautiful body shines like a blue lotus.
His form enchants the minds of gods,
humans, and sages.

मस्तक तिलक, अलक घुंघराले।
आओ कृष्ण बांसुरी वाले।।

Mastak tilak, alak ghungraale.
Aao Krishna bansuri wale.

He has a tilak on his forehead, and his
hair is curled in rings.
Come, O Krishna, the one with the flute.

करि पय पान, पूतनहि तार्यो।
अका बका कागासुर मार्यो।।

Kari pay paan, Pootnahi taarayo.
Aka baka kaagasur maarayo.

He drank the poison from Putana and destroyed her.
He killed Agha, Baka, and Kakasura (evil demons).

मधुवन जलत अगिन जब ज्वाला।
भै शीतल लखतहिं नंदलाला।।

Madhuvan jalaat agin jab jwala.
Bhai sheetal lakhathin Nandalala.

When the fire of the burning forest of
Madhuban was raging,
The sight of Nandalala made the fear
vanish, and everything became calm.

सुरपति जब ब्रज चढ्यो रिसाई।
मूसर धार वारि वर्षाई॥

Surapati jab Braj chadhyo risai.
Moosar dhaar waari varshai.

When the king of the gods became angry and ascended the Braj,
He poured down a shower of rain in the form of a storm.

लगत लगत व्रज चहन बहायो।
गोवर्धन नख धारि बचायो।।

Lagat lagat vraj chahan bahaayo.
Govardhan nakh dhaari bachayo.

As the rain poured down, it flooded the village,
But Lord Krishna lifted the Govardhan Hill with his finger and saved them all.

लखि यसुदा मन भ्रम अधिकाई।
मुख मंह चौदह भुवन दिखाई।।

Lakhi Yasuda man bhram adhikaai.
Mukh man choudah bhuwan dikhai.

When Yashoda saw this, her mind became more confused,
And she saw all fourteen worlds within his mouth.

दुष्ट कंस अति उधम मचायो।।
कोटि कमल जब फूल मंगायो।।

Dusht Kans ati udham machayo.
Koti kamal jab phool mangayo.

The wicked Kansa created great turmoil,
And when he called for a million lotuses
as an offering.

नाथि कालियहिं तब तुम लीन्हें।
चरण चिह्न दै निर्भय कीन्हें।।

Naathi Kaaliyahi tab tum leenhe.
Charan chihn dai nirbhay keenhe.

Then you defeated the serpent Kaliya,
Leaving your footprints and making the
world fearless.

करि गोपिन संग रास विलासा।
सबकी पूरण करी अभिलाषा॥

Kari gopina sang raas vilasa.
Sabki pooran kari abhilasha.

You danced the divine Raas with the Gopis,
And fulfilled all their desires.

केतिक महा असुर संहार्यो।
कंसहि केस पकड़ि दै मार्यो।।

Ketik maha asur sanhaaryo.
Kansahi kes pakad dai maarayo.

You killed many great demons,
And when you caught Kansa by the hair,
you destroyed him.

मात-पिता की बन्दि छुड़ाई।
उग्रसेन कहं राज दिलाई।।

Maat-pita ki bandi chhudaai.
Ugrasen kahin raaj dilai.

You freed your parents from captivity,
And restored the throne to Ugrasena, your grandfather.

महि से मृतक छहों सुत लायो।
मातु देवकी शोक मिटायो।।

Mahi se mrtak chhahoon sut laayo.
Maatu Devaki shok mitayo.

You brought back the six dead sons of
your mother,
And removed the grief from Devaki's
heart.

भौमासुर मुर दैत्य संहारी।
लाये शट दश सहसकुमारी।।

Bhaumasur mur daitya sanhaari.
Laaye shat dash sahasakumaari.

You destroyed the demon Bhaumasur,
And brought with you sixteen thousand princesses.

दै भीमहिं तृण चीर सहारा।
जरासिंधु राक्षस कहं मारा।।

Dai bheemahin trin cheer sahaara.
Jarasingh rakshas kahin maara.

You gave support even to the weak,
And killed the demon Jarasandh.

असुर बकासुर आदिक मार्यो।
भक्तन के तब कष्ट निवार्यो।।

Asur Bakaasur aadik maarayo.
Bhaktan ke tab kasht nivaarayo.

You killed the demons like Bakasur and others,
And removed the troubles of your devotees.

दीन सुदामा के दुख टार्यो।
तंदुल तीन मूंठ मुख डार्यो।।

Deen Sudama ke dukh taarayo.
Tandul teen moonth mukh daarayo.

You alleviated the suffering of Sudama,
And gave him three handfuls of rice,
filling his mouth.

प्रेम के साग विदुर घर मांगे।
दुर्योधन के मेवा त्यागे।।

*Prem ke saag Vidur ghar maange.
Duryodhan ke mewa tyaage.*

Vidur asked for simple greens,
While Duryodhan offered him lavish food,
but he rejected it.

लखी प्रेम की महिमा भारी।
ऐसे श्याम दीन हितकारी।।

Lakhi prem ki mahima bhaari.
Aise Shyam deen hitkaari.

Seeing the immense glory of love,
Such is Lord Shyam, who is the
benefactor of the poor.

भारत के पारथ रथ हांके।
लिये चक्र कर नहिं बल थाके।।

Bharat ke Parath rath haanke.
Liye chakra kar nahin bal thaake.

Bharat, the driver of the chariot, urged it forward,
But Krishna, with his wheel, did not tire or lose strength.

निज गीता के ज्ञान सुनाए।
भक्तन हृदय सुधा वर्षाए।।

Nij Geeta ke gyaan sunaye.
Bhaktan hriday sudha varshaaye.

He imparted the knowledge of his own Geeta,
And showered the nectar of wisdom in the hearts of his devotees.

मीरा थी ऐसी मतवाली।
विष पी गई बजाकर ताली।।

Meera thi aisi matwaali.
Vish pee gayi bajakar taali.

Meera was so devoted and intoxicated with love,
She drank poison and clapped her hands in joy.

राना भेजा सांप पिटारी।
शालीग्राम बने बनवारी।।

Rana bheja saanp pitari.
Shaligram bane Banwari.

The king sent a snake in a box,
But Krishna turned it into a Shaligram,
the eternal deity.

निज माया तुम विधिहिं दिखायो।
उर ते संशय सकल मिटायो॥

Nij maya tum vidhihin dikhayo.
Ur te sanshay sakal mitayo.

You showed the world your divine magic,
And removed all doubts from the hearts
of the people.

तब शत निन्दा करि तत्काला।
जीवन मुक्त भयो शिशुपाला।।

Tab shat ninda kari tatkaala.
Jeevan mukt bhayo Shishupala.

After facing a hundred insults, Shishupala was freed from life, his soul liberated.

जबहिं द्रौपदी टेर लगाई।
दीनानाथ लाज अब जाई।।

*Jabhin Draupadi ter lagayi.
Deenanath laaj ab jaayi.*

When Draupadi cried out for help,
The Lord of the poor removed her shame.

तुरतहि वसन बने नंदलाला।
बढ़े चीर भै अरि मुंह काला।।

Turathahi vasan bane Nandalala.
Badhaye cheer bhay ari muhn kaala.

At once, Lord Krishna made her clothes appear,
And the enemy's face turned black in disgrace.

अस अनाथ के नाथ कन्हइया।
डूबत भंवर बचावइ नइया।।

As anath ke naath Kanhiya.
Doobat bhawar bachavi naiyaa.

Krishna is the Lord of the helpless,
He saves those drowning in the whirlpool
of life.

'सुन्दरदास' आस उर धारी।
दया दृष्टि कीजै बनवारी।।

'Sunderdas' aas ur dhaari.
Daya drishti keejai Banwari.

With faith in his heart, Sunderdas prays, 'Grant your merciful sight, O Lord of the forest.'

नाथ सकल मम कुमति निवारो।
क्षमहु बेगि अपराध हमारो।।

Naath sakal mam kumati nivaaro.
Kshamahu beegi apradh hamaaro.

O Lord, remove all my ignorance,
And forgive my sins swiftly.

खोलो पट अब दर्शन दीजै।
बोलो कृष्ण कन्हइया की जै।।

Kholo pat ab darshan deejai.
Bolo Krishna Kanhiya ki jai.

Now open the veil and grant me your vision,
Let us chant the victory of Krishna, the beloved Kanhiya.

यह चालीसा कृष्ण का, पाठ करै उर धारि।
अष्ट सिद्धि नवनिधि फल, लहै पदारथ चारि।।

*Yah Chalisa Krishna ka,
paath karai ur dhaari.
Asht siddhi nav nidhi phal,
lahe padarth chaari.*

This Chalisa of Krishna, when recited with devotion,
Bestows the eight siddhis, nine treasures, and the four fruits of life.

श्री कृष्ण आरती

आरती कुंजबिहारी की, श्री गिरिधर कृष्णमुरारी की
गले में बैजंती माला, बजावै मुरली मधुर बाला।
श्रवण में कुण्डल झलकाला, नंद के आनंद नंदलाला।
गगन सम अंग कांति काली, राधिका चमक रही आली।
लतन में ठाढ़े बनमाली;
भ्रमर सी अलक, कस्तूरी तिलक, चंद्र सी झलक;
ललित छवि श्यामा प्यारी की।।
श्री गिरिधर कृष्णमुरारी की।।

आरती कुंजबिहारी की, श्री गिरिधर कृष्ण मुरारी की।।
आरती कुंजबिहारी की, श्री गिरिधर कृष्ण मुरारी की।।

कनकमय मोर मुकुट बिलसै, देवता दरसन को तरसैं।

गगन सों सुमन रासि बरसै;
बजे मुरचंग, मधुर मिरदंग, ग्वालिन संग;
अतुल रति गोप कुमारी की।।
श्री गिरिधर कृष्णमुरारी की।।

आरती कुंजबिहारी की, श्री गिरिधर कृष्ण मुरारी की।।
आरती कुंजबिहारी की, श्री गिरिधर कृष्ण मुरारी की।।

जहां ते प्रकट भई गंगा, कलुष कलि हारिणि श्रीगंगा।
स्मरन ते होत मोह भंगा;
बसी सिव सीस, जटा के बीच, हरै अघ कीच;
चरन छवि श्रीबनवारी की।।
श्री गिरिधर कृष्णमुरारी की।।

आरती कुंजबिहारी की, श्री गिरिधर कृष्ण मुरारी की।।
आरती कुंजबिहारी की, श्री गिरिधर कृष्ण मुरारी की।।

चमकती उज्ज्वल तट रेनू, बज रही वृंदावन बेनू।

चहुं दिसि गोपि ग्वाल धेनू;
हंसत मृदु मंद,चांदनी चंद, कटत भव फंद;
टेर सुन दीन भिखारी की।।
श्री गिरिधर कृष्णमुरारी की।।

आरती कुंजबिहारी की, श्री गिरिधर कृष्ण मुरारी की।।
आरती कुंजबिहारी की, श्री गिरिधर कृष्ण मुरारी की।।

आरती कुंजबिहारी की, श्री गिरिधर कृष्ण मुरारी की।।
आरती कुंजबिहारी की, श्री गिरिधर कृष्ण मुरारी की।।

Shri Krishna Aarti

Aarti Kunj Bihari Ki
Shri Girdhar Krishna Murari Ki
Gale Mein Baijanti Mala,
Bajave Murali Madhur Bala.
Shravan Mein Kundal Jhalakala,
Nand Ke Anand Nandlala.
Gagan Sam Ang Kanti Kali,
Radhika Chamak Rahi Aali.
Latan Mein Thadhe Banamali;
Bhramar Si Alak, Kasturi Tilak,
Chandra Si Jhalak;
Lalit Chavi Shyama Pyari Ki.
Shri Girdhar Krishna Murari Ki.

Aarti Kunj Bihari Ki,
Shri Girdhar Krishna Murari Ki.
Aarti Kunj Bihari Ki,
Shri Girdhar Krishna Murari Ki.

Kanakmay Mor Mukut Bilse,
Devata Darsan Ko Tarse.
Gagan So Suman Raasi Barse;
Baje Murchang, Madhur Mridang,
Gwaalin Sang;
Atual Rati Gop Kumaari Ki.
Shri Girdhar Krishna Murari Ki.

Aarti Kunj Bihari Ki,
Shri Girdhar Krishna Murari Ki.
Aarti Kunj Bihari Ki,
Shri Girdhar Krishna Murari Ki.

Jahaan Te Pragat Bhayi Ganga,
Kalush Kali Haarini Shri Ganga.

Smaran Te Hot Moh Bhanga;
Basi Shiv Shish, Jataa Ke Beech,
Harei Agh Keech;
Charan Chhavi Shri Banvaari Ki.
Shri Girdhar Krishna Murari Ki.

Aarti Kunj Bihari Ki,
Shri Girdhar Krishna Murari Ki.
Aarti Kunj Bihari Ki,
Shri Girdhar Krishna Murari Ki.

Chamakati Ujjawal Tat Renu,
Baj Rahi Vrindavan Benu.
Chahu Disi Gopi Gwaal Dhenu;
Hansat Mridu Mand, Chandani Chandra,
Katat Bhav Phand;
Ter Sun Deen Bhikhaaree Ki.
Shri Girdhar Krishna Murari Ki.

Aarti Kunj Bihari Ki,
Shri Girdhar Krishna Murari Ki.
Aarti Kunj Bihari Ki,
Shri Girdhar Krishna Murari Ki.

Aarti Kunj Bihari Ki,
Shri Girdhar Krishna Murari Ki.
Aarti Kunj Bihari Ki,
Shri Girdhar Krishna Murari Ki.

Shri Krishna Aarti

The *Aarti* of Kunjbihari, the Lord
Giridhara, Krishna Murari,
With a garland of *Vaijayanti* around His
neck, He plays the sweet flute.
In His ears, the shining earrings sparkle,
the joy of Nand, Nandalala.
His form shines like the sky, His
complexion is dark,
Radhika's glow is dazzling,
He stands as a gardener, His locks like a
bee, His forehead adorned with musk,
His face like the moon,
The charming beauty of beloved
Shyama (Radha).
Shri Giridhara Krishna Murari.

Aarti of Kunjbihari,
Lord Giridhara, Krishna Murari

The *Aarti* of Kunjbihari, the Lord
Giridhara, Krishna Murari,
The *Aarti* of Kunjbihari, the Lord
Giridhara, Krishna Murari.

Golden peacock crown shines,
the gods yearn to see Him.
From the sky, flowers rain down,
The *murchang* (musical instrument) plays,
the sweet *mridang* (drum) sounds,
with the cowherd girls,
In incomparable love, the
gopis dance with Him.

Shri Giridhara Krishna Murari.

Aarti of Kunjbihari, Lord Giridhara, Krishna Murari

The *Aarti* of Kunjbihari, the Lord
Giridhara, Krishna Murari,
The *Aarti* of Kunjbihari, the Lord
Giridhara, Krishna Murari.

Where Ganga first appeared,
the remover of sin, Shri Ganga.
By remembering Him,
all attachment is destroyed,
He resides on Lord Shiva's head, amidst
His locks, washing away all sin,
The foot-glow of Shri Banwari (Krishna).

Shri Giridhara Krishna Murari.

Aarti of Kunjbihari, Lord Giridhara, Krishna Murari

The *Aarti* of Kunjbihari, the Lord
Giridhara, Krishna Murari,
The *Aarti* of Kunjbihari, the Lord
Giridhara, Krishna Murari.

The shining sands on the banks sparkle,
the flute of Vrindavan plays.
In all directions, the cowherds
and cows roam,
The soft breeze blows gently, the
moonlight shines,
The bonds of worldly life are cut,
Listening to the call of the humble beggar.

Shri Giridhara Krishna Murari.

Aarti of Kunjbihari, Lord Giridhara,
Krishna Murari

The *Aarti* of Kunjbihari, the Lord
Giridhara, Krishna Murari,
The *Aarti* of Kunjbihari, the Lord
Giridhara, Krishna Murari.

Aarti of Kunjbihari,
Lord Giridhara, Krishna Murari

The *Aarti* of Kunjbihari, the Lord
Giridhara, Krishna Murari,
The *Aarti* of Kunjbihari, the Lord
Giridhara, Krishna Murari.